谷仓神秘事件

Mystery in the Barn

[美]威力·布莱文斯/著　　[美]吉姆·帕约/绘

王婧/译

电子工业出版社·

Publishing House of Electronics Industry

北京·BEIJING

本书中文简体版专有出版权由Red Chair Press LLC通过CA-Link International LLC授予电子工业出版社，未经许可，不得以任何方式复制或抄袭本书的任何部分。

版权贸易合同登记号　图字：01-2022-0735

图书在版编目（CIP）数据

谷仓神秘事件 / (美) 威力·布莱文斯 (Wiley Blevins) 著；(美) 吉姆·帕约 (Jim Paillot) 绘；王婧译. -- 北京：电子工业出版社，2023.6
（胖狗和瘦狗）
ISBN 978-7-121-44941-3

Ⅰ.①谷… Ⅱ.①威…②吉…③王… Ⅲ.①儿童故事－图画故事－美国－现代 Ⅳ.①I712.85

中国国家版本馆CIP数据核字(2023)第077358号

责任编辑：范丽鹏
印　　刷：天津图文方嘉印刷有限公司
装　　订：天津图文方嘉印刷有限公司
出版发行：电子工业出版社
　　　　　北京市海淀区万寿路173信箱　邮编：100036
开　　本：787×1092　1/16　印张：26.25　字数：264千字
版　　次：2023年6月第1版
印　　次：2023年6月第1次印刷
定　　价：208.00元(全8册)

凡所购买电子工业出版社图书有缺损问题，请向购买书店调换。若书店售缺，请与本社发行部联系，联系及邮购电话：(010) 88254888，88258888。
质量投诉发邮件至zlts@phei.com.cn，盗版侵权举报请发邮件至 dbqq@phei.com.cn。
本书咨询联系方式：(010) 88254161 转 1862，fanlp@phei.com.cn。

目 录

闪亮登场的主角们

克鲁德

艾克

绒球小姐

鲍勃

出大事儿了!

　　对克鲁德和艾克来说，这又是美好而快乐的一天。他们在院子里欢快地奔跑着，跳跃着，汪汪大叫着，不过当他们跑到马丁太太院子的围栏附近时……
　　"快停下来!"克鲁德大喊。

"为什么呀?"艾克问。

"地上有泥巴。"克鲁德说。

"哦，对呀，"艾克说，"幸好有你。"

这时，绒球小姐跳到了围栏上面，她浑身发抖，好像刚刚看到了什么非常恐怖的东西似的。

"我们要不要问问她怎么了？"艾克说。

"别问了。"克鲁德说。绒球小姐又开始抖了起来。

"好吧好吧，"克鲁德问，"你到底怎么了？"

绒球小姐低哼一声："我以为你永远不会问呢！有件大事儿就要发生啦！"

这时，马丁太太院子后面的谷仓里突然发出一阵嘈杂的声音。

"你刚才是从谷仓那边过来的吗？"艾克问。

"哦，我是绝对不可能出现在那种地方的，"绒球小姐说，"有身份的猫都不会的。"

"那声音听上去像是我们的地方，"克鲁德急忙说，"快走，艾克。那里要出大事儿了！"

克鲁德和艾克说完立马翻过围栏——啪叽！

"我们怎么扭头就给忘了呢！"克鲁德抱怨道。

克鲁德和艾克甩掉身上的泥巴，朝着谷仓的方向，往山下跑去。突然他们脚下一个"急刹车"，停在一扇大红门面前。

　　克鲁德和艾克把耳朵贴在大门上，突然，大门被一阵低沉又响亮的"哞哞"声震得直摇晃。"会是什么呀？"艾克问，"一匹马？"

　　"不是。"克鲁德回答。

　　这时，大门又被一阵刺耳的"哼哼"声震得直摇晃。"会是什么呀？"艾克问，"一只鸡？"

　　"不是。"克鲁德回答。

　　最后，大门再次被一阵刺耳的"咯咯"声震得直摇晃。"会是什么呀？"艾克问道，"一群大象？"

　　"不是。"克鲁德回答，"但是一定有什么大事儿要发生了！"克鲁德问艾克："我们要不要进去？"

　　"我都听你的。"艾克说。

　　"那我们就进去吧。"克鲁德说。

克鲁德轻轻地推开了谷仓的大门。突然，里面响起一声尖叫。

艾克被吓呆了："我们**真的**要进去吗？"

"谷仓里能出什么事儿呢？"克鲁德反问。

艾克深吸一口气，然后躲在克鲁德的身后，蹑手蹑脚地走了进去。突然……

谷仓里正在数身上斑点的奶牛猛地停了下来，卷尾巴的猪也不再卷尾巴了，忙着擦鸡蛋的母鸡也不再擦蛋了。

这时，一只老鼠忽然从木桶后面探出头来。

9

"只是围栏那边的两只狗而已，"老鼠说，"警报解除。"于是，谷仓里的动物又继续做自己的事，有哞哞叫的，有哼哼哼的，还有咯咯咯的，一切又都恢复到了没人到访时的样子。

"那我们现在做什么呢？"艾克问。

"我们去问问有没有人知道，即将发生的那件大事。"

克鲁德和艾克慢悠悠地走到了一群奶牛面前。"哞哞，你好。"其中一只奶牛打着招呼。"哞哞，你也好！"艾克说。

"你知道接下来会发生什么大事吗？"克鲁德问。奶牛点了点头，然后朝着猪圈指了指。

于是克鲁德和艾克又溜到猪圈旁边。"哼哼，你好。"其中一只猪打着招呼。"哼哼，你也好！"艾克说。

"你知道接下来会发生什么大事吗？"克鲁德问。

就在这时，所有的猪都开始哼哼叫起来，他们绕着猪圈跑啊跑，但是没有一只猪回答克鲁德的问题。

　　"好吧，"克鲁德有点失望，"那我们还是去问问母鸡们吧。"

　　"好的，"艾克说，"母鸡总是什么都知道。"

　　"咯咯，咯咯，咯咯哒。"一群母鸡吵吵嚷嚷地打着招呼。"咯咯，咯哒，你也好！"艾克说。

　　"你们知道接下来会发生什么大事吗？"克鲁德问。

　　"知道，"其中一只母鸡说，"但是我们的公鸡不见了，在他回来之前，我们什么也不能告诉你。"

咯咯，咯咯哒，
救命啊！

"那我们现在能做点什么？"艾克问。

"那我们就好好地探索一下谷仓吧，"克鲁德说，"这样还可以打发一下时间。"

克鲁德和艾克开始在谷仓里尽情地奔跑，每一间牛棚都要探头进去瞧一瞧。他们跳过一堆木桶，跃过几把铁铲，又从一群老鼠的头顶上飞了过去，最后爬上梯子，扑通一声跳到干草垛上。

"这也不能打发多长时间啊，"艾克说，"所以，我们现在还能做点什么呢？"

"我有主意了，"克鲁德说，"咱们来玩躲猫猫的游戏吧。"

"好呀好呀，"艾克开心地说，"我最喜欢玩躲猫猫的游戏了，那你打算怎么来玩这个游戏呢？"

"我来躲，"克鲁德说，"然后你数10个数字，等你数完了，就开始找我。"

"明白。"艾克说。克鲁德趁着艾克捂住眼睛的时候，悄悄地溜走藏了起来。"1……2……3……8……16……97……33……81……82……10。"

艾克睁开了眼睛，大声喊："我来喽！"艾克看看
这儿，瞧瞧那儿，抬头看看，低头看看，又向四周看了
看，但就是没有看到克鲁德的踪影。于是，他又回到了
干草垛上。

"这个游戏没有克鲁德可真是一点意思也没有！"
艾克不高兴地抱怨道。

这时，艾克突然感觉身下的草垛里有什么东西在动，"嘭！"克鲁德大叫一声从草垛里蹦了出来。

　　"啊——"艾克尖叫起来，"你吓得我差点灵魂出窍了！"说完，他一下跳到克鲁德身上，在草垛上滚了起来，他们滚啊滚啊滚，直到……

　　"咯咯，咯咯哒，救命啊！"声音是从谷仓里面传来的。

　　"会是谁呀？"艾克问。

　　"是其中一只母鸡，"克鲁德说，"咱们快去看看究竟出什么事儿了。"

坐好，坐好，哎哟！

克鲁德和艾克顺着梯子爬下来，向着鸡群跑了过去。

"就快到时候啦，就快到时候啦！"一群母鸡吵吵嚷嚷地大喊着。她们六神无主地跑来跑去，嘴里不停地咯咯哒、咯咯哒、咯咯哒地叫着。

克鲁德抓住其中一只母鸡的翅膀，瞪着母鸡圆圆的小眼睛，问道："到底发生了什么大事？"

母鸡指了指地上满满两窝鸡蛋说："公鸡是他们的爸爸，可他还没有回来。"母鸡继续说："我们要一起出去把他找回来，所以，能不能请你们先帮忙坐在鸡蛋上，然后等我们回来呀？"

"我们可喜欢坐着了。"艾克说。

"没错，"克鲁德表示同意，"这件事儿就交给我们吧。"

于是俩人坐在了鸡蛋上。可没过多一会儿，艾克就感觉自己屁股底下突然晃了一下，他叫了一声："哦，我的天哪！"

　　克鲁德感觉自己屁股底下突然被拱了一下，他开心地说："这感觉可真有趣啊！"

　　紧接着，俩人的屁股底下这被戳一下，那被捅一下，戳一下，捅一下。"哎哟！"克鲁德和艾克大喊一声。

俩人从鸡窝上跳了下去，回头朝下一看，鸡窝里全是一只只嫩黄色的小鸡。

　　"叽叽。" 一只小鸡叫着。

　　"吉普？"艾克纳闷道。

　　"叽叽，叽叽，叽叽。"其他小鸡跟着叫了起来。有一只小鸡蹦到了鸡窝边上。

　　"你是我们的爸爸吗？"小鸡问。

　　"爸爸？"艾克反问。

　　"不不不，"克鲁德急忙说，"咱们快跑。"

克鲁德和艾克从谷仓里冲了出来，他们爬上山，翻越过围栏，最后回到了自家的院子里。

　　"回家的感觉可真好呀。"艾克说。

　　"是的，"克鲁德说，"没有**大事**发生的地方才是
最好的地方啊！"

　　"晚安了，哥们儿！"

　　"晚安！"

英文原文

Meet the Characters

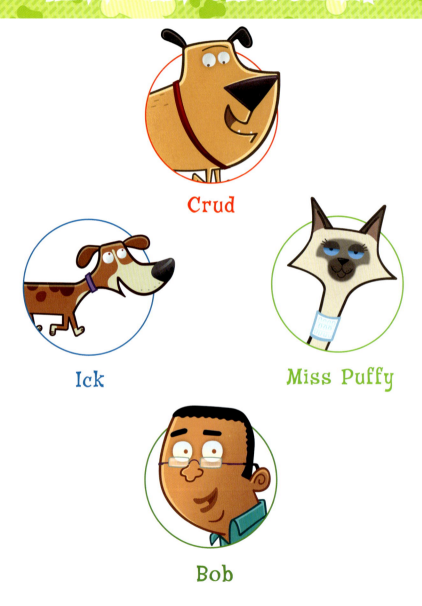

Crud

Ick

Miss Puffy

Bob

Something Big!

Ick and Crud set out to have another fun day. They raced through their yard, skipping and yapping until they came to Mrs. Martin's fence.

"Stop," yelled Crud.

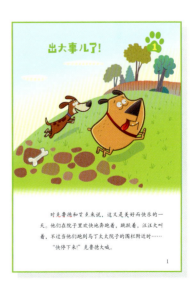

出大事儿了!

时克鲁德和艾克来说，这又是美好而快乐的一天。他们在院子里欢快地奔跑着、跳跃着，汪汪大叫着，不过当他们跑到马丁太太院子的围栏附近时……
"快停下来!" 克鲁德大喊。

1

"我们要不要问问她怎么了？"艾克说。

"别问了。"克鲁德说。绒球小姐又开始抖了起来。

"好吧好吧，"克鲁德问，"你到底怎么了？"

绒球小姐低哼一声："我以为你永远不会问呢！有件大事儿就要发生啦！"

这时，马丁太太院子后面的谷仓里突然发出一阵嘈杂的声音。

"为什么呀？"艾克问。

"地上有泥巴。"克鲁德说。

"哦，对哟，"艾克说，"幸好有你。"

这时，绒球小姐跳到了围栏上面，她浑身发抖，好像刚刚看到了什么非常恐怖的东西似的。

"Why?" asked Ick.

"The mud," said Crud.

"Oh, right," said Ick. "Good thinking."

Miss Puffy hopped on top of the fence. She shook like she had just seen something very scary.

"Should we ask?" asked Ick.

"No," said Crud. Miss Puffy shook again. "I give up," said Crud. "What's bugging you now?"

Miss Puffy purred. "I thought you'd never ask. Something BIG is about to happen."

Just then a noise rang out from the barn in the back of Mrs. Martin's yard.

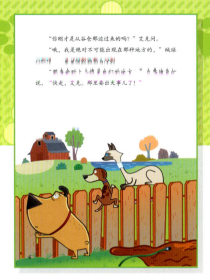

"你刚才是从谷仓那边过来的吗？"艾克问。

"哦，我是绝对不可能出现在那种地方的，"绒球
小姐说。"有教养的猫咪都不会那样。"

"那看来那儿是我们的地方，"卡鲁德说，
说，"快走，艾克。那里要出大事儿了！"

"Did you just come from the barn?" asked Ick.

"Oh, I wouldn't be caught dead in the barn," said Miss
Puffy. "No classy cat would."

"Then it sounds like our kind of place," said Crud. "Let's go,
Ick. Something big is about to happen there!"

2

What Could Go Wrong?

Ick and Crud jumped over the fence. Splat!

"How soon we forget," moaned Crud.

He and Ick shook off the mud, then raced down the hill and to the barn. They skidded to a stop at the big, red door.

能出什么事儿呢？

2

克鲁德和艾克说完立马翻过围栏——啪叽！

“我们怎么扭头就给忘了呢！”克鲁德抱怨道。

克鲁德和艾克甩掉身上的泥巴，朝着谷仓的方向，往山下跑去。突然他们脚下一个“急刹车”，停在一扇大红门面前。

5

克鲁德和艾克把耳朵贴在大门上，突然，大门被一阵低沉又响亮的"哞哞"声震得直摇晃。"会是什么呀？"艾克问，"一匹马？"

"不是。"克鲁德回答。

这时，大门又被一阵刺耳的"哼哼"声震得直摇晃。"会是什么呀？"艾克问，"一只鸡？"

"不是。"克鲁德回答。

最后，大门再次被一阵刺耳的"咯咯"声震得直摇晃。"会是什么呀？"艾克问道，"一群大象？"

"不是。"克鲁德回答，"但是一定有什么大事儿要发生了！"克鲁德问艾克："我们要不要进去？"

"我都听你的。"艾克说。

"那我们就进去吧。"克鲁德说。

6 — 7

They leaned their ears against the door. A loud, low moo shook it. "What is that?" asked Ick. "A horse?"

"No," said Crud.

Then a squealing oink shook the door. "What is that?" asked Ick. "A chicken?"

"No," said Crud.

Finally, a chorus of squawks shook the door. "What is that?" asked Ick. "A bunch of elephants?"

"No," said Crud. "But something big is going on! Should we?" asked Crud.

"I will if you will," said Ick.

"Then let's go inside," said Crud.

Crud nudged open the barn door. A screech shot out.

Ick froze. "Do we *really* have to go inside?" he asked.

"What could go wrong in a barn?" asked Crud.

Ick gulped. He hid behind Crud as they tiptoed inside. Suddenly…

The cows stopped counting their spots. The pigs stopped curling their tails. And the chickens stopped polishing their eggs.

A mouse poked her head out from behind a barrel.

"只是围栏那边的两只狗而已,"老鼠说,"警报解除。"于是,谷仓里的动物又继续做自己的事,有哞

"It's just those two dogs from over the fence," she said. "All clear." So, the animals went back to mooing, oinking, squawking, and doing what animals do in a barn when no one is watching.

"What do we do now?" asked Ick.

"Let's see if someone knows the big thing that is about to happen."

So Ick and Crud shuffled over to the cows. "Moo," said one of the cows. "Poo to you, too," said Ick.

"Do you know what is about to happen?" asked Crud. The cow nodded and pointed to the pigpen.

于是克鲁德和艾克又溜到猪圈旁边。"哼哼，你好。"其中一只猪打着招呼。"哼哼，你也好！"艾克说。

"你知道接下来会发生什么大事吗？"克鲁德问。

就在这时，所有的猪都开始哼哼叫起来，他们绕着猪圈跑啊跑，但是没有一只猪回答克鲁德的问题。

"好吧，"克鲁德有点失望，"那我们还是去问问母鸡们吧。"

"好的，"艾克说，"母鸡总是什么都知道。"

"咯咯，咯咯，咯咯哒。"一群母鸡吵吵嚷嚷地打着招呼。"咯咯，咯哒，你也好！"艾克说。

"你们知道接下来会发生什么大事吗？"克鲁德问。

"知道，"其中一只母鸡说，"但是我们的公鸡不见了，在他回来之前，我们什么也不能告诉你。"

So Ick and Crud skipped over to the pigs. "Oink," said one of the pigs.

"Boink to you, too," said Ick.

"Do you know what is about to happen?" asked Crud.

All the pigs began to squeal and run around the pen. But not one answered Crud.

"Okay," said Crud. "Let's ask the chickens."

"Yes," said Ick. "The chickens always know what's going on."

"Cluck, cluck, squawk," shouted the chickens.

"Click, clack, squeak to you, too," said Ick.

"Do you know what is about to happen?" asked Crud. "Yes," said one of the chickens. "But we are missing our rooster. We can't tell you until he comes back."

3

Cluck, Squawk, Help!

"What do we do now?" asked Ick.

"Let's explore the barn," said Crud. "That will pass the time."

Ick and Crud ran through the barn, stuck their heads in every stall, hopped over buckets, leaped over shovels, jumped over mice, then climbed up the ladder, and plopped onto the hay.

"That didn't take long," said Ick. "So, what do we do now?"

"I know," said Crud. "Let's play hide-n-seek."

"Yes," said Ick. "That's my favorite game. How do you play hide-n-seek again?"

咯咯，咯咯哒，救命啊！

"那我们现在能做点什么？"艾克问。

"那我们就好好地探索一下谷仓吧，"克鲁德说，"这样还可以打发一下时间。"

克鲁德和艾克开始在谷仓里尽情地奔跑，每一间牛棚都要探头进去瞧一瞧，他们跳过一堆木桶，跃过几把铁锹，又从一群老鼠的头顶上飞了过去，最后爬上梯子，扑通一声跳到干草堆上。

14

"这也不能打发多长时间啊，"艾克说，"所以，我们现在还能做什么呢？"

"我有主意了，"克鲁德说，"咱们来玩躲猫猫的游戏吧。"

"好呀好呀，"艾克开心地说，"我最喜欢玩躲猫猫的游戏了，那你打算怎么来玩这个游戏呢？"

15

"I will hide," said Crud. "Then you count to ten. When you're done, you look for me."

"Got it," said Ick. He covered his eyes as Crud snuck away to hide. "1… 2… 3… 8… 16… 97… 33… 81… 82… 10."

Ick opened his eyes. "Here I come," he yelled. Ick looked here. Ick looked there. He looked up. He looked down. And he looked all around. But he didn't find Crud. He plopped back onto the hay.

"This game is not fun without Crud," he moaned.

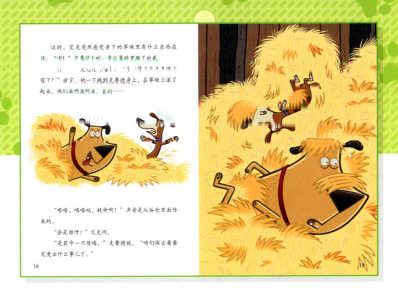

这时，艾克突然感觉身下的草垛里有什么东西在动。"吼！"克鲁德大叫一声从草垛里蹦了出来。

"啊！"又把艾克吓了一跳。"你把我都吓尿裤子了！"说完，他一下跳到克鲁德身上，在草垛上滚了起来，他们滚啊滚啊滚，直到……

"咯咯，咯咯哒，救命啊！"声音是从谷仓里面传来的。

"会是谁呀？"艾克问。

"是其中一只母鸡，"克鲁德说，"咱们快去看看究竟出什么事儿了。"

18   19

Then he felt something move in the hay. "BOO!" yelled Crud, as he popped out.

"AAAAAGGGGHHHH!" screamed Ick. "You scared the doggie bones out of me." Then he jumped on Crud and rolled in the hay. They rolled and rolled and rolled until…

"Cluck, squawk, HELP!" rang out from inside the barn.

"Who is that?" asked Ick.

"One of the chickens," said Crud. "Let's go find out what's wrong."

4

Sit, Sit, Ouch!

Ick and Crud climbed down the ladder and raced to the chickens.

"It's about to happen! It's about to happen!" yelled all the chickens. And they ran around and around clucking and clacking and squeaking and squawking.

Crud grabbed one of them by the wings. He looked the chicken in its beady eyes. "What is about to happen?" he asked.

The chicken pointed to two nests filled with eggs. "The rooster is their daddy. He isn't back," the chicken said. "We must all go find him. Can you sit on the eggs until we get back?"

"We like to sit," said Ick.

"Yes," said Crud. "We'll do it."

坐好，坐好，哎哟！

克鲁德抓住其中一只母鸡的翅膀，瞪着母鸡圆圆的小眼睛，问道："到底发生了什么大事？"

母鸡指了指地上满满两窝鸡蛋说："公鸡是她们的爸爸，可他还没有回来。"母鸡继续说："我们要一起出去把他找回来，所以，能不能请你们先帮忙坐在鸡蛋上，然后等我们回来呀？"

"我们可喜欢坐着了。"艾克说。

"没错，"克鲁德表示同意，"这件事儿就交给我们吧。"

克鲁德和艾克顺着梯子爬下来，向着鸡群跑了过去。

"就快到时候啦，就快到时候啦！"一群母鸡叽叽喳喳地大喊着。她们六神无主地跑来跑去，嘴里不停地咯咯哒、咯咯哒、咯咯哒地叫着。

20

21

于是俩人坐在了鸡蛋上。可没过多一会儿，艾克就感觉自己屁股底下突然晃了一下，他叫了一声："哦，咦咦咦咦咦！"

克鲁德感觉自己屁股底下突然被拱了一下，他开心地说："这感觉可真有趣啊！"

紧接着，俩人的屁股底下这被戳一下，那被捅一下，戳一下，捅一下。"哎呦！"克鲁德和艾克大喊一声。

22

23

The two sat on the nests. But before long… Ick felt a wiggle under his butt. "Oh, my," he said.

Crud felt a squiggle under his butt. "This feels funny," he said.

Then each felt a poke. And another poke. Poke. Poke. Poke. "Ouch!" yelled Ick and Crud.

They hopped off the nests and looked down to see two nests filled with little yellow chicks.

"Peep," said one of the chicks.

"Jeep?" asked Ick.

"Peep, peep, peep," said the other chicks. Then one little chick hopped on the edge of the nest.

"Are you our daddy?" the chick asked.

"Daddy?" asked Ick.

"Oh, no," said Crud. "Run!"

克鲁德和艾克从谷仓里冲了出来，他们爬上山，翻越过围栏，最后回到了自家的院子里。

And they raced out of the barn, up the hill, over the fence, and into their yard.

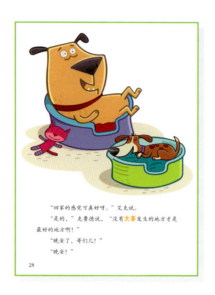

"回家的感觉可真好呀。"艾克说。

"是的，"克鲁德说，"没有大事发生的地方才是最好的地方啊！"

"晚安了，哥们儿！"

"晚安！"

"It's good to be home," said Ick.

"Yes," said Crud. "It's good to be in a place where nothing *big* is about to happen.Goodnight, buddy."

"Goodnight."